Your Vacation Tips, Advice and Planning Guide

By Thomas P. Berns

© Copyright 2013

Table of Contents

Copyright and Disclaimer iii
Chapter 1 – Why Go on a Cruise Vacation? 1
Chapter 2 - Finding the Best Cruise Deals 6
Chapter 3 - Should I use a Travel Agent? 11
Chapter 4 - What is Included in the Cruise Price? 17
Chapter 5 – Types of Cabins on Cruise Ships 24
Chapter 6 - Should I Buy Travel Insurance For a Cruise? 28
Chapter 7 – What to Wear and Things to Pack 34
Chapter 8 – What to Expect on a Cruise Ship 44
Chapter 9 - Avoiding Seasickness While on a Cruise Ship 52
Chapter 10 – Avoiding the Norovirus 57
Chapter 11 – Gambling on Cruise Ships 61
Chapter 12 – Shore Excursions 65
Final Words 70
About the Author 70

Copyright and Disclaimer

Your First Cruise Vacation
Tips, Advice and Planning Guide

Copyright © 2013: Thomas P. Berns
Published: March 2013

No part of this book may be reproduced in any form without permission in writing from the author. Reviewers may quote brief passages in reviews.

Disclaimer

While all attempts have been made to verify the information provided in this publication, neither the author nor the publisher assumes any responsibility for errors, omissions, or contrary interpretations of the subject matter herein.

This book is for entertainment purposes only. The views expressed are those of the author alone, and should not be taken as expert instruction or commands. The reader is responsible for his or her own actions.

Neither the author nor the publisher assume any responsibility or liability whatsoever on the behalf of the purchaser or reader of these materials.

Chapter 1 – Why Go on a Cruise Vacation?

There have been a lot of recent negative incidents concerning the cruise industry of late.

The most tragic is when the Costa Concordia Cruise line was sailing too close to the shoreline and ran aground on a couple of rocks that are typically found in Mediterranean waters off the coast of Tuscany, Italy. What is outrageous about this situation is that the captain went off the normal path and veered too close to the shore because he wanted to "show boat" to the local residents off the Italian coast. It is a disaster that killed 32 people and caused an incredible amount of environmental and ecological damage to the Tuscan coastline.

Other incidents

- The Carnival Triumph (Feb 2013) had to be towed to a port in Mobile Alabama following a fire in the engine room.
- The Carnival Elation (Mar 2013) had to be escorted by a tug boat because of a

mechanical problem with its steering mechanism.
- The Carnival Dream (Mar 2013) experienced power interruptions at the island of St. Maarten in the Caribbean which stranded more than 4,000 passengers.

The above are isolated incidents that are unfortunate but can happen on occasion. The one common denominator is that they are happening to Carnival Cruise Lines, the largest operator in the world. They may feel a financial impact of all this negative publicity which will probably lead to deeper discounts.

However, the relative number of these incidents is small compared to the number of cruises that take place every year. No matter how you travel, there are always horror stories.

How many times do we hear about planes stuck on the tarmac for various reasons? There are many times, particularly in the winter when weather is bad with snow conditions that this occurs. However, no one talks about the possibility of never flying again. You may hear that they won't fly with the same airline, but they'll never say they are not flying ever again.

I'm not sure why it is different on a cruise?

Perhaps we now view flying as a necessity, especially for business travel whereas cruising is a "luxury" or a "non-essential" item?

Whatever the reason may be I wouldn't let that deter you from booking your first cruise and enjoying it to the maximum extent possible. There are risks in everything we do. It's just that these cruise incidents get a lot of publicity when things go awry.

Despite all the recent negative publicity concerning cruise vacations, it is an industry that is growing at approximately 7% per year and it is estimated that in 2013 there will be more than 20 million people that are expected to go on a cruise.

The ships are getting bigger, more luxurious and including more entertainment options and more destinations.

Some of them can carry upwards of 5,000 people on the ship. They are in essence a city on the sea.

If you've never been on a cruise, you may be wondering - why should I go on a cruise? What is so great about it?

Without a doubt a cruise vacation offers you the best value for the money.

When you plan a normal vacation you have to take into consideration and plan for the following components:

- Transportation
- Lodging
- Food
- Entertainment

When you book a cruise all the components above for all practical purposes are taken care of for you! That means you have less planning to do which alleviates a lot of stress. And if you are planning a vacation for the family, this can be a huge burden off your shoulders.

Later in the book I will cover more of this in detail.

Budget

There are also many options you can choose from to accommodate your financial budget. Cruise lines offer many options from 2 day cruises all the way up to one week and more!

And coupled with the different accommodation options available, you can always find the right combination that will work for your budget.

Destinations

When you book a cruise you will have the option of visiting one or more destinations depending on the cruise itinerary. Usually the destinations are very desirable from a vacation point-of-view or the cruise lines wouldn't consider them. In addition these places offer many unique type of experiences like swimming with dolphins or manatees, viewing icebergs, going to a rum factory, zip lining, etc. These experiences are usually not available to you if you were trying to plan and book your own non-cruise vacation. And you don't need to worry about directions since the ship will take you there!

How many days should I book?

For first-timers I would not recommend a one week cruise. I would start out with a 3 or 4 day cruise so you get familiar with the experience. Even though I highly recommend the cruising option as a vacation experience, there are some that prefer other options, even after experiencing a cruise. You may fall into that category, so it's best to start off on "training wheels", so to speak.

Chapter 2 - Finding the Best Cruise Deals

People are always looking for ways to save money and this concept remains true for cruise trip travel. To find the best possible cruise deals, you'll need to do a bit of research as well as utilize a few effective techniques for cutting down costs. In the subsequent sections of this chapter, I will provide you with a few proven ways to find the best cruise deals possible.

Do a Web Search

If you type in the words "Cruise Deals" on a search engine then you will be presented with nearly twenty-five million results. It seems as though that nowadays, more and more websites are providing people with a chance to save money on their cruise fare.

Start with the larger providers like Priceline, Travelocity or Expedia to analyze possible deals. There are other smaller sites as well that have deals. Always make sure that you are dealing with a credible and certified website before handing out personal information like your name, address, or bank account information.

Discount Cruise Sites

There are also sites geared toward the cruise industry that often have special deals. A few of them are Cruise.com, iCruise.com and 1800Cruise.com.

Sign Up For Newsletters

Visit your soon-to-be favorite cruise line's website and sign up for their e-mail newsletter. The popular ones are Carnival, Disney, Holland America, Norwegian and Royal Caribbean. The cruise lines will often reward loyal followers and first-time cruisers by emailing them coupons that provide them with huge discounts on upcoming trips. Subscribing via email takes seconds and in return you will receive constant information about future trips and how to save money.

Are you traveling with a past guest?

If you know someone who previously rode with a certain cruise line then you could be eligible for past-guest savings. Keep in mind that these savings offers will not be available for first-timers boarding the cruise ship.

And the best part is that you will automatically become a part of their past-guest list program once you travel with them a single time. In most cases, they will ask you for your email address so that they can send you discount coupons as well as other promotional offers that you can use for your next trip.

Is there a time when there are more deals available?

Just like every other industry, if you can depart when there is a huge supply available, you can usually secure a good deal. January through March is considered a "wave season" when there are a lot of sailings as residents in northern climates like to get away from the cold weather. Of course there is usually high demand in this period. But the cruise lines know this, so they are usually offering some type of deal or discount during this period if you book far enough in advance.

Another good time of year for the Caribbean is from August, September and October as many people do not like to travel during hurricane season. Luckily the cruise lines can change their itineraries if there is an impending storm that might interfere with the voyage.

Check the Sunday Newspaper

Many times in the Sunday newspaper, particularly in the cities where there are departures (i.e. Miami, Fort Lauderdale, Tampa) along with places like Dallas and Atlanta, there are deals that can be found. Just peruse the Travel Section of the paper and you are sure to find some travel agents that have access to these deals.

Call the Cruise Line Directly

A good way to see if there are any specials on cruise travel is go to directly to the horse's mouth! You can call the cruise lines and tell them your plans and they will offer you a rate. You can then use that rate to comparison-shop against your other options.

Order tickets as far in advance as possible

Generally you can book a cruise even as far as 2 years into the future. Normally the price will be the lowest the farther in the future the cruise is scheduled to set sail. And then the prices will generally creep upward as the time gets closer to departure. Many experts agree that the "sweet spot" of booking a cruise is approximately 6 to 12 months before sailing.

Sometimes if a cruise is under capacity there may be a fare reduction prior to departure to try to fill the ship. Just keep in mind your options will be more limited if you wait until the last minute. However, from a cruise operator's point of view they would rather give you a deal than to have an empty cabin.

Compare Prices

And finally you should compare prices trying to secure the best cruise deals. Since you're trying to find the lowest possible price, do your homework and determine which companies are offering the most cost-efficient fares. Taking the time to do this will take you a long way in regards to showing you which cruise lines are offering competitive rates and which ones aren't.

Travel Agents can be your friend

Another possible way to secure a good deal is to utilize the services of a travel agent. The next chapter will go into more detail.

Chapter 3 - Should I use a Travel Agent?

Probably one of the more effective routes that you can take is to book your cruise is through a travel agent. The reason why is because travel agents will have much more access to cruise line information than you will as they work in the industry day in and day out.

As a result, they will be able to sort through this information to help you find the best possible deals. They also have access to "group rates" that are not advertised on the internet. And you don't need to be part of a group to get these deals. Your travel agent can book other clients or collaborate with other travel agents to utilize the group rate.

Their commission

A travel agent will get paid by the cruise line operator. It will not cost you any more or less to utilize their services.

More Benefits of a Using a Travel Agent

Travel agents not only can save you a lot of money

but they can also provide customers with tons of free incentives, perks, and discounts. In some cases, a good travel agent may even be able to provide you with a cabin upgrade at no extra charge. And to say thank you for choosing their services, they'll often leave a bottle of wine or some other amenity and a "Thank You" card in your room once you board.

They can also ask about your preferences and will be much more likely to find travel dates and options that better suit your needs, schedule and budget. Remember that choosing cruise tickets isn't the same as booking a flight or hotel room.

And since this will be your first time on a cruise ship they can give you some insights based on their own experiences and the experiences of their clients. In other words they can find the right cruise for you and your party. If you are looking for a peaceful vacation, they can steer you away from the cabin that is near the night club. Or if you are prone to sea-sickness, they can arrange to get your cabin located where that would be less likely.

They can also recommend onshore excursions based on what other clients have told them about their own past experiences.

More than likely your cruise will not depart from the city in which you live, therefore, a travel agent can help you with booking a flight and a hotel that you may need prior to your voyage.

And finally, they can offer you a travel insurance policy and explain all the options available to you to protect your investment. Later in the book will be a chapter devoted to travel insurance.

Disadvantages of using a Travel Agent

Of course just like everything else, there are a couple of disadvantages you should be aware of if you decide to use a travel agent.

First of all, the ticket will be considered "their own booking". In order for them to earn a commission, the ticket, for all practical purposes, will be in their name. You will still be able to see the ticket on the cruise operator's website, and it will have your name as a passenger. However, if you need to make any changes, you will have to call your travel agent.

The other disadvantage is that you will need to give them your credit card information, so it is important that you find one that you can trust and hopefully not go out of business. Therefore, it is important to choose the correct one from the start.

How to Find a Travel Agent

So if you do make the decision of booking your trip through a travel agent then there are a few effective ways to go about choosing one.

Start with your own friends and family members. You should see if there are any travel agents that they recommend. If you utilize Facebook or Twitter you can ask your friends or followers who they recommend. You can also do an internet search for those that are in your area and check their reviews online. If you live in Detroit a Google search with the phrase "Travel Agents Detroit" would yield a lot of listing in your area. Or even better yet do a search for "Cruise Travel Agents Detroit" and see what results are from this more specialized query.

You can also check the travel section of your Sunday newspaper along with the Yellow Page listings.

Make sure that your travel agent has the proper credentials, training and experience to their name.

You should inquire about any certification classes that they have taken as well as make sure that they are established under the BBB (Better Business Bureau) and ASTA (American Society of Travel Agents). This will lessen your chances of finding a bad one.

Knowledge and Experience

How much experience and knowledge does your particular travel agent have regarding cruising in general? To figure this out, you should be asking them a lot of questions. Find out how many cruises they have personally been on as well as ask about how long they've been a travel agent. If you can find a travel agent who is particularly savvy about a cruise in a region that you're interested in then this could be a good reason for choosing their services.

Destination-Specific Cruises

Sometimes you will run into travel agents who specialize in certain types of cruises. For example, you may encounter someone who can help you book a Caribbean cruise but not a European one. While there is nothing wrong with this, you want to make sure that their specialty matches your wants and needs regarding your cruise destination.

During the Interview

Once you have allocated a travel agent that you are exceptionally interested in, you shouldn't be afraid to ask them questions. During the initial interview, they will be asking you a lot of questions as well. More specifically, they'll want to know more about your preferences, lifestyle, budget, and schedule. From here, they will go through their database and find a cruise that best suits all of those areas.

Chapter 4 - What is Included in the Cruise Price?

While cruises are extremely popular for many people all around the world, not many of us understand all of the costs that go into paying for a cruise. More specifically, a lot of travelers and vacationers aren't entirely sure what's included in their trip and what is not. With that being said, here is a breakdown of the price components of a cruise:

Basic Cost of Cruise

This is considered the "base" amount of money that you pay and will include

- Accommodations (Your Cabin)
- Ship Transportation
- Most Meals
- Most Beverages
- Entertainment
- Swimming Pool Use

Port Fees and Taxes

Although a lot of people don't realize it, they will need to pay a relatively large sum of money in port fees and taxes. This money usually goes towards something known as "parking fees", which is basically the cost of having the ship docked at a certain station. And depending on the government, a "head tax" may also be imposed on travelers. You will pay this amount directly to the cruise line. They will in turn pay the port fees and taxes on your behalf.

Reading a Cruise Advertisement

When you are reading a cruise advertisement, realize that you probably won't be paying the exact amount that is on the promotional flyer. There is a lot hidden in the fine print that most people don't see. Let's take a look at what a few of those areas are:

Lead-In Pricing: This is the part of the ad that is designed to catch your eye. However, it typically isn't the full amount that you're going to pay for your cruise trip. Also keep in mind that if you do end up paying close to the lead-in price that you'll have had to have done it quickly because these rooms tend to go quite fast.

Fine Print: The fine print section of a cruise advertisement can easily add a few hundred dollars to the total cost of a cruise. However, be thankful that the government plays a huge role in restricting the amount of leverage that cruise lines have using this tactic.

Get the complete price

When you are shopping for your cruise vacation it is a good idea to get the complete price that includes taxes, port charges, etc. That way you can use it as a comparison. The cruise lines themselves are pretty good about publishing the complete fare on their websites.

What is typically not included in the base fare?

The following OPTIONAL items are items that you will need to pay out of your own pocket:

- Gambling (however it is free to enter a casino)
- Alcoholic Beverages
- Alternate Dining

- Spa and Massage Services
- Internet access
- Photographs (from the ship photographer)
- Laundry
- Phone Calls
- Gift Shop Purchases
- Art Auctions
- Video Arcade
- Shore Excursions

In addition, tipping and gratuities are not included in the price of the cruise so make sure you include gratuities to your cabin steward and dining staff. There are suggested guidelines located in your ship's brochure. You have the option to prepay for your gratuities but I typically do not do that. Some people say you get better service when you do, but I have not found that to be the case.

The good thing about cruises is that you will be able to charge most of the above items to your room. And then at the end of the journey you will get an itemized listing and settle your account, similar to a stay at a hotel.

Which cruise line should I choose?

Back in the day cruising was a concept for the ultra-rich. The only time the common man could afford any type of sea voyage might have been when they crossed over from Europe and landed at Ellis Island to start a new life in the United States.

These days, mostly in large part to Carnival Cruise Lines, the idea of taking a cruise vacation has become a lot more mainstream and affordable.

However, there still are differences depending on which cruise line you choose as some of them have a very specific clientele that they cater to.

Here is a breakdown of the most popular cruise lines along with links to their website information and phone numbers (United States):

Most popular, most affordable

Carnival
http://www.Carnival.com
800-327-9501

Norwegian (NCL)
http://www.ncl.com
800-327-7030

Royal Caribbean
http://www.royalcaribbean.com
800-398-9819

These are perfect for first-time cruisers along with seniors, singles, those traveling with families, etc. These tend to be the most affordable.

Middle of the road cruise lines, a bit more pricey:

Celebrity
http://www.celebritycruises.com/home.do
800-722-5941

Disney
http://disneycruise.disney.go.com/
800-370-0097

Holland America
http://www.hollandamerica.com/main/Main.action
800-426-0327

MSC
http://www.msccruises.com
877-956-1622

Princess
http://www.princess.com/
800-421-0522

Disney is of course famous for catering to those with families and children.

Holland America caters to an older, more established clientele. Consequently, they will have less night-time activities aboard their ships.

The higher-end cruise lines include the following:

Azamara
http://www.azamaraclubcruises.com/
877-999-9553

Crystal
http://www.crystalcruises.com/
888-722-0021

Oceania
http://www.oceaniacruises.com/
800-531-5619

Paul Gauguin
http://www.pgcruises.com/
(800) 848-6172

Regent Seven Seas
http://www.rssc.com/
800-505-5370

Seabourn
http://www.seabourn.com/main/Main.action
800-929-9391

Silversea
http://www.silversea.com/
800-722-9955

Windstar
http://www.windstarcruises.com/
800-258-7245

Chapter 5 – Types of Cabins on Cruise Ships

Cabins come in all kinds of shapes, sizes, and styles. And each one will have their own unique set of amenities. With that being said, expect your cabin to be about half the size of a hotel room. One thing that the cruise lines excel at is making use of every single nook and cranny.

You'll typically have a single bed, a closet, a bathroom with shower, a desk, a television, and maybe a small area for sitting or eating. They can also combine 2 beds for a couple or split them apart for single travelers. Now, living arrangements can be enhanced if you pay for them and in most cases, the more luxury cabins will have two rooms- one for sleeping and one for relaxing.

Aside from choosing the type of cruise that you would like to be a part of, you'll need to make the very important decision of choosing your cabin. Keep in mind that this is the only part of the ship that you will have to yourself so you want to be sure that it's something that accommodates well and you know what you are getting.

The cruise lines don't make it easy to choose as there could be as many as 200 different options when you factor in location and size.

But don't let that worry you. Essentially, there are only basically the five types of accommodations that follow below from least expensive to most expensive. Keep in mind that each cruise line will have its own "lingo" as to how they list these in their brochures or websites.

Inside Cabins

These tend to be the most cost-efficient types of cabins available. This is because they are located towards the center of the ship and they have no windows. However, you may still be able to see a spectacular view via the room's television.

Also take note that although these rooms tend to be the least expensive of all the different types of cabins, they still come with all of the amenities that you would ever need including storage, television, a bathroom and shower, and beds.

If you are claustrophobic or prone to sea sickness you may want to consider the more expensive options below.

Ocean View Cabins

While ocean view cabins aren't necessarily larger than inside cabins, they house a view with a porthole (a bit bigger than the window on an airplane) where you can view the ocean. Ocean view cabins will contain the same basic amenities as inside cabins and maybe a few "extras". If you want an amazing view but don't want to spend an arm and a leg on balcony cabins then this is the ideal route to take.

Balcony Cabins

If you're interested in having your own private balcony while on board a cruise ship then balcony cabins are the way to go. However, do realize that they are more expensive. But if the sound of enjoying your breakfast on an early morning on your balcony sounds appetizing then balcony cabins might just be worth the price.

Mini-Suites

Mini-suites, while not available on all cruise ships, consist of a living area as well as a sleeping area. They also tend to have slightly better amenities than regular homes like larger shower areas and even couch and chairs.

Regular Suites

Finally, we have regular suites, which typically consist of two rooms that contain luxurious items. These are the most expensive items that you will find on board a cruise ship and they provide tons of features and amenities.

Aside from the extra space, you'll be fixed with lounge chairs, an extra balcony, and a hot tub. And in most cases you will be rewarded with extra "perks" that include having access to a private pool and lounge area as well as given special meals during your visit at restaurants.

Chapter 6 - Should I Buy Travel Insurance For a Cruise?

Travel insurance is something that can provide a lot of benefits but also something that can be a relatively large expense. With that being said, your main priority before departing is to figure out if travel insurance is something that you will actually need.

First off, realize that travel insurance is a backup plan against bad scenarios that are unlikely to happen. However, there still are a lot of things that can go wrong on your cruise including the following:

- You can miss the boat

- You can lose your luggage

- Your luggage can get destroyed

- You can have an unexpected medical emergency at sea

- You can have an unexpected medical emergency prior to leaving

- You or your travel companion(s) may unexpectedly pass-away

- Your flight to the port was delayed

- Your cruise operator can go out of business

- Your ship's plans can be rerouted

Do You Need Travel Insurance?

This is a question that you will ultimately need to answer yourself. Typically, the larger the investment in the cruise, the more likely you will want to purchase travel insurance. The longer you are waiting for your voyage, the more likely something can change in your plans where you may need to cancel. For example, if you are booking a cruise for travel one year from now, there are more things that can change than if you are booking a voyage for the following week. If you are a parent, you also know that if you are traveling with children, there are more likely to be cases where your plans may change.

Contact Your Current Homeowners or Renters Insurance Company

A lot of people don't realize that their current homeowners (or renters) insurance company may provide some type of coverage for their travels. This can be incredibly useful, especially if you are worried about protecting valuable items like laptops and smartphones.

Call your Credit Card Company

Many credit card companies will also offer some type of travel insurance if you book the travel with their credit card. Some of them will include it without your knowledge as a free benefit. Other times you will have to purchase additional coverage.

Types of Travel Insurance

There are **comprehensive policies** that cover everything from financial default to medical insurance. And there are also policies that are very specific in their coverage. You have to read the fine print to make sure you know what you are purchasing.

Here are the most common types of insurance coverage:

Health & Medical Insurance – Many health insurance companies, including Medicare, do not cover medical related costs when you are overseas.

Evacuation – covers the cost of medically evacuating you by helicopter or jet so you can receive medical attention.

Cancel for Any Reason – this will have an expensive price tag, so it is best to ensure your plans are set before you may want to purchase this one.

Trip Interruption – when you begin your trip but you are unable to finish it.

Financial Default – in case the cruise line or any of the other operators declares bankruptcy.

Flight Insurance – in case the airline crashes when you are traveling to your port of departure.

Adventure Sports or Extreme Sports – if you plan on sky diving or bungee jumping, then you may want to purchase this coverage. Your normal health insurance coverage will typically exclude these types of activities.

Where to buy Travel Insurance

- Travel Agent

If you do decide to use a travel agent like mentioned in a previous chapter, they can also offer you a policy and explain your various options. This is another good reason to use a travel agent.

- Travel Insurance Company

There are also companies that offer travel insurance. Your best bet would be to find a travel insurance company that specializes in providing customers with cruise specific travel insurance. If you'd like to find a list of reputable companies that can provide people with travel insurance then visit the official webpage of the Travel Insurance Association.

http://www.ustia.org/

- The Cruise Line

Many cruise line operators also offer travel insurance. If you are booking your trip directly with the cruise line you should inquire about the travel insurance options. They tend to be a little bit more expensive than and not as comprehensive as other policies you may find. The good thing is that you can purchase it during the booking process.

Compare Policies

Once you have found a few companies that you may be interested in, compare their prices until you find the one that best suits your budget. Comparing as many policies as possible is the best way to separate the ones that serve you from the ones that don't.

Best Time to Buy Travel Insurance

The best time to buy travel insurance is when you make your initial deposit. Of course you can purchase it right up to the date of your voyage. However, you will generally get a better deal the earlier you can purchase it. And you will have more chance to utilize it if something unexpected does indeed happen.

The Price Factors

The price of the travel insurance policy will also be determined by the price of the voyage (your financial investment) and your age.

Chapter 7 – What to Wear and Things to Pack

One of the more common questions that people have when boarding a cruise ship is what items to bring and which ones to leave at home. In other words, how the heck are we supposed to pack?

With that being said, I've dedicated a chapter of this book to showing you what you need to know. Below, I'll show you how to successfully pack and prepare for a cruise.

What Items Are Necessary?

First off, realize that certain items will be necessary. They include:

- Medications
- Cruise Line Tickets
- Change of Clothes
- Important Documents (I.D., Passport, etc.)

These are usually the bare minimum that you would be able to get away with and still survive on board a cruise ship. But if you would really like to make your trip exceptionally special, keep reading to learn more about how to properly pack and prepare.

Do I need a passport?

The short answer to this question is yes. The real answer is not necessarily.

In theory, whenever you leave the country (assuming you are traveling from the US) you will need a passport to re-enter. However, the US now allows an exception for cruise travel if your travel falls under what is called a "closed-loop" exception.

This means if you leave from a US port (let's say Miami) enter a foreign country (let's say Mexico) and re-enter the same port (Miami), then you are exempt from the passport requirements. However you will need a Driver's License along with a CERTIFIED copy of your Birth Certificate.

However, I would not recommend traveling without a passport. Your options for using your credit card will diminish because some merchants will want to see it if you are making a purchase. And then what happens if you get sick on the cruise and have to be air-lifted to a foreign hospital? What happens if you get so drunk that you miss the cruise departure from the port-of-call? In those scenarios, it would be a lot tougher to re-enter the United States if you were without a passport.

Therefore, I always recommend carrying one. In addition, it's a good idea to have a copy of it in your suitcase in case the actual one gets lost while you are in port.

If you are from the United Kingdom, you will definitely need to travel with a passport.

Check the Dress Code

Each ship will have its own dress code but basically there will be a dress code that is appropriate during the day and one for dining at night.

The dress code during the day is usually very lax with shorts, T-shirts, collared shirts and beach attire all being appropriate.

At night the situation is different, especially if you want to dine in the main restaurant during your assigned time.

Depending on the length of the cruise, you may have one, two, or even more "formal" nights where some lines even require a tuxedo. This would be more typical on a higher-end cruise line like Holland America. Some will offer tuxedo rentals.

And the rest of the dinners may be more "semi-formal" and relaxed which would require suit and tie for the guys and eveningwear for the ladies.

If you are not up for the formal dining experience, you are always free to dine by yourself at one of the other restaurants.

Women's Attire

In regards to activities during the day, females on-board should be wearing shorts that are comfortable jeans, pants, and skirts. Activities that take place outdoors require bathing suits and other casual apparel like poolside cover-ups. On nights that are cooler than usual, women should bring long scarfs and sweaters to stay warm.

Men's Attire

Men should bring a few days' worth of casual wear as well as a few days of formal wear or business casual attire for the dinner meal depending on the cruise ship guidelines. Button-down shirts are very versatile and can serve well for both categories. Men should also consider bringing khaki pants as these can also serve as both casual and formal wear. Finally, bringing one suit and tie can work wonders in regards to visual appearance for social events on-board.

Suggestions for Specific Destinations

Depending on where you will be travelling, you'll need to pack slightly differently. For example, if you are travelling to the Caribbean then you should consider packing a small waterproof jacket during their rainy season. If you're going to be traveling in the waters of Northern Europe later in the year then you should pack for chilly nights and wear plenty of removable layers. Finally, make sure that you bring hats, glasses, sunblock, and any other items that will protect you from the sun in exceptionally hot locations.

Check your Cruise Operator's Website

Since there are so many different cruise lines, it is best to check the website for your particular cruise line as each one will have different policies regarding the dress code.

Workout Gear

If you plan on utilizing the gym, make sure you bring your workout attire.

Other Items to Consider

A lot of cruise lines will recommend that you bring an outlet strip if you plan on charging multiple items at once. The reason why is because most cruise lines only offer one or two outlets per room, which can make charging multiple electronic devices extremely difficult.

Cell Phones, Electronics, Laptops, etc.

Also make sure that you inquire about the Wi-Fi rates that are offered on board your cruise. These can typically be quite expensive so items like laptops and smartphones shouldn't be expected to be used that often, unless you plan on spending a lot of money on roaming and Wi-Fi charges. And depending on your destination you will more than likely lose cell phone coverage when you are in the middle of the Gulf of Mexico or Caribbean.

Camera

Don't forget to bring you camera or video recorder to photograph those special moments. There are more tips about photography in the next chapter below.

Small Backpack or Tote Bag

It's also a good idea to carry a small backpack or a tote bag for when you are docked at portside.

Toiletries

The ship will often provide their own soap and shampoo though dispensers located in the bathrooms of the ship. They will also have a small hair dryer available. However, you should pack your own if you have any preferences or are prone to rashes from using new soaps, shampoos, etc.

Don't forget to bring your toothbrush, toothpaste, dental floss, etc.

And if you do forget to bring something, the ship will have mostly everything you would need available for sale.

Sea Sickness Medicine

If you are prone to sea sickness it's a good idea to talk to your doctor prior to your journey. There are prescription medicines available along with over-the-counter medicines that have shown to be very effective. The ship will usually have some available free of charge. It is in their best interests that their guests enjoy themselves.

Sunscreen

It's always a good idea to carry some sunscreen, particularly if you are cruising to a southern location like the Caribbean or if the beach will be your destination.

Comfortable Shoes

Flip-flops are a must especially when you are by the

pool; however, if you plan on doing some hiking excursions, you ought to bring your own hiking shoes.

Other items to consider

- Hats
- Books
- Magazines
- Sunglasses
- Binoculars
- Journal

The following items should NOT be brought on the ship:

- Firearms
- Weapons
- Chemicals
- Explosives
- Illegal Drugs
- HAM Radios
- Fireworks or Explosives
- Irons and ironing boards

Alcoholic Beverages – these are not allowed for consumption. If you purchase any alcohol from any of the ports-of-call or from the ship's own store they will store it for you and have it available at the end of the voyage.

They used to be more lenient in allowing alcohol on board but now they rely heavily on alcohol sales to make a profit. As you can imagine, alcohol sales and the casino are a huge money maker for the cruise lines.

Chapter 8 – What to Expect on a Cruise Ship

As you walk through the cruise ship doors for the first time, you may be wondering what will be waiting for you on the other side. As a first time traveler upon one of these vessels then you may feel overwhelmed with all of the new scenery and living arrangements. With that being said, it is essential that you learn about what to expect on a cruise ship so that you can better enjoy your time on them.

Arrival

Once you arrive to board the ship, you'll most likely be approached by a photographer who will ask you to pose for a picture. You don't have to purchase the picture right then and there but it will be available as a purchase option later on down the road. As you can imagine the prices are a bit on the high side. These photographers will be available all throughout the cruise to photograph your vacation activities. You can usually be photographed alongside some props that make it look like a fun experience. It is considered bad manners to use your digital camera to photograph yourself with the props. Leave that for the professional ship photographers as they are trying to make a living with their craft.

From there, a staff member will ask for your boarding card as well as I.D. and other important documents.

You will also go through security although it is not as extensive as taking off your shoes at the airport. Your luggage will also go through X-ray screening and the amount of liquids that you can carry on board will be limited to the same travel restrictions as airline travel.

If there is any suspicion that you are carrying anything illegal on board, your luggage will be set aside for further inspection.

You also have the option to transport your luggage to your room or you can leave it with the handlers and they will transport it to your room where it will be available later in the day, usually in a couple of hours.

You will also be given a questionnaire or asked verbally if you are experiencing any flu-like symptoms or had any flu-like symptoms during the past 3 days. It is important that you answer honestly. Viruses can quickly spread among passengers when it is confined to a closed-quarter environment like a ship. If there is any question about your health, you will probably be examined by the ship's physician and they can deny you from boarding if they feel you would be a risk to other passengers.

Your Card

You will also be given a card that will be tied to your room number and credit card along with your passport information. You will need this whenever you are conducting "money" transactions as any purchases will be tied to the card. This will act as your currency so you don't have to carry around actual cash. This works great when you are at the pool and want to grab a drink. At the end of the cruise you will be given your statement and will have the chance to dispute any charges that are inaccurate. You will then of course have to settle your account.

This (your card) will also be needed to leave the ship when it arrives at your port-of-call or final destination. You will also need it to get back onto the ship. This is how the ship keeps track of how many people are remaining on the ship and how many are off-ship.

Your card serves as another important function: It will also serve as your room key. As you can see, this card becomes very important, so don't lose it!

Muster (Safety) Drill

Before the ship sets sail, or very early in the cruise, the ship director will have everyone practice something known as a "Muster Drill". This is basically a drill that will help people know what to do and where to go in the case of an emergency. This is a mandatory drill.

In most cases, there will be signs on the back of the cabin doors that will direct people on where to go once these sirens sound. Once you have arrived to that location, you will be dismissed by a staff member and be allowed to roam freely once again.

Entertainment

This will be the highlight of your cruise trip and should be something to look forward to. Entertainment is something that will be completely subjective depending on the specific cruise line that you have taken. However, you should expect the following:

* Mini Concerts (Live Music)

* Magic Shows

* Stand-Up Comedy - Nothing beats a good laugh while out at sea. Keep in mind that only certain cruise lines will offer comedy shows.

* Day-Time Performances

* Night Clubs - The majority of cruise lines offer a variety of night clubs to choose from. These are

perfect for having fun, drinking, and socializing with the other guests on board. Some of them will even have live music.

These live shows will house all kinds of performers and performances including singers, dancers, and even the occasional magician. There are even cruise lines that have their very own built-in movie theater where guests can watch Hollywood grade movies free of charge. Some even have ice skating rinks.

Gyms and Spas: These are perfected for health-based individuals who would like to relax as well as remain in peak physical condition while on vacation. They also offer (for a fee) massages, facials, pedicures and other types of spa treatments.

Access to the gym is usually included in the cost of the trip. It is very inspiring to work out or run on a treadmill as you look out on the horizon and see the open waters.

And some will even have a "jogging track" on the upper deck. You'll have to be careful as other passengers will be on the track walking or milling around with no particular purpose.

The Food

Finally, expect to partake in a lot of eating and drinking as you'll probably have access to a various buffets with tons of delicious finger food, pizza, salad bar and dessert. Just do keep in mind that you will need to pay extra money for alcoholic beverages while on board.

Usually you will have an option of American, Asian, Italian, Mexican and Latin Cuisine.

Buffets are available for breakfast, lunch and dinner. For these options you are free to dine when you want, where you want, and with whom you want.

For dinner, you have the option of a sit-down service complete with a wait-staff service. The restaurant usually has a maître d' and provides some sort of entertainment during dinner. You will be assigned to a table and your dinner mates will be the same throughout your journey (unless you arrange a trade with another party).

This is one of the best features of a cruise is that you can eat what you want at a time of your choosing. The meals are usually set during a range of hours but there is usually something available to eat pretty much 24/7. And you don't have to wash the dishes!

Chapter 9 - Avoiding Seasickness While on a Cruise Ship

Seasickness is something that can cause someone to experience vomiting, cramps, and nausea while on board a ship at sea. And for most people, these symptoms can be detrimental to the fun and excitement that is supposed to be experienced on board a cruise ship.

What is Seasickness?

First off, motion sickness is caused when outer forces are competing against the body's natural balancing system. This is often why rough seas can leave people feeling less than optimal when on a cruise ship. Fortunately, there are proactive techniques that can be utilized to lessen seasickness symptoms as well as prevent them from occurring in the first place.

Prescription Medications

There are certain drug-based remedies that actually do a good job at lessening the symptoms associated with seasickness. Most of the more effective ones come in the form of patches that are designed to be placed directly behind the ear.

They typically last for eight hours and can be an efficient solution that can last for a few days. Do keep in mind that most of the stronger remedies are only available by prescription so make sure that you consult your local physician about acquiring some.

Never take any medication that you have not been prescribed as possible side effects can include dizziness, blurry vision, and dry mouth.

Over-The-Counter Drugs

If you'd like to take medications that aren't quite as strong and that don't require a prescription then you can choose over-the-counter seasickness drug solutions. Here are a few of the more common brands that should work quite effectively:

- Meclizine
- Dramamine
- Benadryl

There are certain cruise lines that will dispense

these medications freely and there are others that will sell them to you on board. Either way, make sure that you look into this before getting on board. You should always consult your doctor prior to taking any medications (prescription or over-the-counter) as it may react with your current medication. You may have a medical condition that would preclude you from taking these medicines.

Alternate Remedies

If you aren't someone who isn't necessarily fond of taking drugs to feel better then there are other, drug-free remedies that you can utilize. One relatively popular route that a lot of people take is wearing Sea-Band wristbands.

They are very comfortable to wear and will work by actively preventing you from experiencing the side-effects associated with seasickness. These bands can be purchased at most major drug stores.

Another proven method for alleviating nausea on a cruise ship is to take in ginger-based products. The great part about ginger-based solutions is that it can be taken in many different forms including:

- Candy
- Pill
- Tea
- Powder

And although it isn't scientifically confirmed, some people suggest that eating green apples upon leaving the docking station should help eliminate some of the symptoms of seasickness. Some ships do offer green apples as part of their room service menus.

Other Considerations

In order to fully acclimate yourself to being on the cruise ship, it is important that you spend as much time as possible on the upper decks. Focusing on the horizon will force your body to regain its equilibrium. In regards to booking a room, try to book your cabin towards the middle of the ship and on the lower levels as this is the area of the vessel that will experience the least amount of sway.

You should also keep in mind that when the weather

is unpleasant, more people than normal will experience sea-sickness. When the weather is pleasant sea sickness is not a problem for most people. Most of the time you will not even know you are on a vessel. And then there will be moments when you feel the movement of the ocean. It is sometimes similar to walking down the aisle on an airplane in flight.

Chapter 10 – Avoiding the Norovirus

Not only has there been mechanical issues plaguing the cruise industry of late, there have also been cases where viruses can quickly spread among the crew and passengers aboard a ship. A common virus is the Norwalk Virus or also known as the Norovirus.

The Norovirus is a virus that can cause gastroenteritis which is an inflammation of the stomach and the large intestines. It is similar to food poisoning; however, it can be spread via contaminated food or water along with physical contact, shaking hands, and even via air. It can also be spread via fecal matter which is why it is super important to wash your hands after changing your baby's diaper.

How long does it last?

The effects of the virus are generally felt within 12 to 24 hours and can last for 2 to 3 days. The effects are not generally life-threatening but the symptoms will leave you feeling very unpleasant for a few days. It can be more life-threatening to children, the elderly and those with weakened immune systems.

What are the symptoms?

The symptoms are typically flu-like in nature and can include the following: nausea, vomiting, diarrhea, stomach cramps, chills and fever.

What should I do if I get infected?

You should visit the ship's doctor and follow their course of action. And also drink plenty of fluids as it can leave you dehydrated. Since it is a viral infection, antibiotics will not work for this one.

Does this happen only on cruise ships?

No, the Norovirus can happen anywhere there are closed quarters including hospitals, dormitories, office buildings, casinos, theaters, etc. When these cases happen on a cruise ship they get a lot of media attention and notoriety because the cruise lines are required to report these cases when over 2% of the passengers are infected. They are required to report these cases to the Centers for Disease Control (CDC) in Atlanta.

What can I do to prevent it?

Washing your hands often with hot water and soap is one of the best ways to prevent many flu infections. You should also avoid any uncooked food and tap water. It is always a good idea to drink bottled water especially if you are visiting places like Mexico and even places that are not notorious for

"Montezuma's Revenge". It's better safe than sorry. It's also a good idea to carry a hand sanitizer around with you. You can find these at your local drug store and they are usually in a few ounce container. You just put a little gel on your hands and rub it in.

What do ships do to prevent this?

Before you board onto your cruise you will be given a questionnaire asking if you have experienced any flu-like symptoms in the last 3 days. If your health is in question, the cruise can deny boarding for fear that you may infect other passengers. They do not like these outbreaks to occur and do everything they can to avoid them. Unfortunately there are probably a few people that lie when they fill out the questionnaire.

It's a tricky situation because if you paid for a cruise and planned a vacation no one likes to alter their plans if they feel like they are "not that sick". This is another good reason to purchase travel insurance prior to your trip as they may cover the cancellation if it is due to illness. As always, read the fine print of your policy.

Will the cruise lines reimburse me if there is an outbreak?

They are not required to reimburse their passengers but many will a refund or give you credit for future travel. Or they can do a combination of the above.

Chapter 11 – Gambling on Cruise Ships

When on a cruise ship, you'll often be bombarded with various forms of entertainment. These forms of entertainment can include dancing, drinking, social gatherings, and event concerts. And the best part is that these entertainment specials will vary from cruise ship to cruise ship so you'll almost always experience something different if you are an avid traveler at sea. With that being said, this section of this guide will highlight entertainment and gambling options on board cruise ships.

Disney Cruise Lines

Keep in mind that Disney Cruise Lines does not offer gambling as an entertainment option as they are geared towards those with family and children.

Should you gamble while at sea?

Initially, a lot of people may feel uncomfortable at the thought of gambling while out at sea. And while most people view this as entertainment, keep in mind that you will lose in the long run, just as you would with any other kind of casino. Just like in Las Vegas, the odds will favor the house.

However, there are instances when people on board walk out with much more money than they walked in with. It is this possibility that encourages the passengers to bring their chips back for higher and better action.

Are gambling cruise ships legal?

The moment that your cruise ship crosses international waters, the casinos will be ready for customers - and a lot of eager ones at that. That is about 12 miles from port.

What is the minimum age to gamble?

This will vary by cruise line, but usually you must be 18 or 21 years of age.

So, what makes gambling on a cruise ship so different from risking your money in other parts of the world?

Well for one, you're on board a cruise ship and that means that you're going to receive high-quality service from dealers and other staff members within the casino. It is likely that you could be complimented, even if you haven't risked a significant amount of money.

Even if you don't know how to play, they usually have tutorials that can teach you. Or the dealer can often teach you on the spot. The staff tends to be more relaxed than what you would find in Las Vegas.

Keep in mind there are daily limits as to the cash that you can receive from the cashier. It is typically capped at about $2,000 per day.

Now many cruise lines are trying to lure some of the more big-time gamblers by compensating their journey with a free cruise. I think some of these big-time players may be exempt from the daily cash requirement.

Since cruise ships are not governed by US laws, they are not as regulated as a casino in Las Vegas, for example. Although it's not published, many claim the odds are not as good as in Las Vegas.

But the cruise lines also realize that happy customers turn into repeat customers. So the odds must not be atrocious or they will lose business.

What games do they have?

They all usually have slot machines along with the typical card tables that you would find in your normal casino. These can include Blackjack along with Caribbean Poker, Texas Holdem, Roulette, Craps, etc. The tables usually start at $5 to enter during the day and can get higher during prime time hours.

Final Advice for Gambling

Just like if you were to gamble in a casino in Las Vegas, it is best to set aside a budget and consider it entertainment. That way, if you do end up losing a lot of money, it won't ruin the rest of your vacation.

Chapter 12 – Shore Excursions

Exploring glaciers, swimming with dolphins, or hiking through ancient cities- these are a few of the adventures that you can partake in when you sign up for shore excursions. Simply put a shore excursion is an activity or set of activities that takes place off of the ship, typically where the ship has been docked.

These are optional and not included in the price of the cruise.

One reason why a cruise line may offer shore excursions is to further increase their profits as well the total length of their port visit. The following sections will provide you with more information on what to expect from shore excursions.

What to Expect

Since different cruise lines will offer different types of land-based tours and attractions, you'll almost always experience something different. Some excursions require active participation like hiking or biking while others fall under the category of "sightseeing" activities. Food tasting, trips to museums, and sailboat rides would all be considered sightseeing excursions.

How Long Do Excursions Last?

The length of a shore excursion will typically vary from activity to activity and cruise line to cruise line. In general, most excursions will be broken up into two categories: half-day excursions and full-day excursions.

Many times lunch will be included with the excursion. However, there are times when it is not, so you must make sure before you book your excursion.

If you're really interested in making the most of your land-based journey then it is highly recommended that you participate in a full-day tour. However, if you're interested in only spending three or four hours participating in an activity then sign up for a half-day excursion.

Where do you book these excursions?

On board there is usually an excursion desk that will help you book your excursion. Many of the newer ships will allow you to book it on their interactive television set, similar to ordering a pay-per-view movie.

Guided Tours vs. Free Roaming

So, how much freedom are you going to have on your shore excursion? Well, this answer really depends on the type of excursion that you're taking. For example, if your excursion involves a trip to a museum then it is likely that you'll be guided by a tour specialist.

Likewise, if your shore excursion simply involves an area that doesn't require a tour guide then you can roam freely and then meet back up with the ship at a later time. Make sure that you inquire about this information before signing up for a shore excursion.

Other Important Considerations

There are some excursions that are going to involve dabbling in a multitude of activities while there are others that will place their focus on one. The one that you end up choosing should be dependent on your own personal preferences.

For example, how many attractions can you handle seeing within any given day?

Do you prefer in-depth tours?

Or do you prefer major highlights of specific areas?

These are a few questions that you should be asking before making any final decisions. Finally, remember that shore excursions tend to fill up quickly so it is important that you sign up for them as quickly as possible. This will guarantee you a spot in the excursion as well as potentially help you snag a lower price.

A word about the operators

Most of the folks that operate these excursions are local businesses or tour guides that do NOT work for the cruise line company. They have, however, been vetted and must meet strict requirements in order to associate themselves with the cruise line. If they do a good job, you should also leave a little tip as a token of appreciation.

You do not have to use the excursions recommended by the ship. There are others onshore that also offer excursions, but you are taking a risk if you utilize their services as they have not been vetted by the cruise line.

And you do not need to do any type of excursion if you do not want to. You are free to stay on the ship and enjoy the ship activities, meals, etc.

And you are also free to roam around on your own when the ship is in port.

Final Words

I hope I've been able to convey all the information necessary for you to make your decision about your first cruise. Or better yet, I hope you have already have made up your mind that you are going to book your first voyage! If you are like me, you will soon discover that it is the best vacation experience ever. You can get up <u>when</u> you want. You can eat <u>what</u> you want. You can eat <u>when</u> you want. You can decide to be entertained or you can just do a lot of nothing. Either way, the choice is yours!

As they say in France...Bon Voyage!

About the Author

Mr. Berns is an entrepreneur and an avid travel writer living in Florida. He just recently discovered the joy of cruising and has been on many since his maiden voyage. He is a proponent of the environment, the nudist lifestyle and enjoys spending his time at the beach and with his dog.

Another book by Thomas P. Berns

Florida Nude Recreation Guide
Beaches, Resorts, Cruises, Festivals and More!
http://www.amazon.com/dp/B009RBK4VS

Thank you

Before you go I'd like to say thank you from the bottom of my heart for purchasing my eBook. I know there are countless other books on this topic but yet you chose mine and I am truly humbled.

If you enjoyed this book, I need your help!

Please take a moment to leave a review for this book on the site where it was purchased.

And if you can also share it with your friends on Facebook and Twitter it would be greatly appreciated as well!

Happy Cruising!

Thomas P. Berns

Manufactured by Amazon.ca
Acheson, AB